DIY SHAMPOO SECRETS

Unlock the Natural Beauty of Your
Hair with Homemade Shampoos –
Recipes, Tips, and Tricks for
Healthy, Organic Tresses

Adams .U. Morris

TABLE OF CONTENTS

CHAPTER 1

Homemade Shampoo

In our fast-paced, modern world, the quest for natural alternatives and sustainable living has gained tremendous momentum. It's no wonder that this movement has extended to the realm of personal care, particularly hair care. The idea of crafting homemade shampoo might initially sound quaint, even antiquated, in a world dominated by mass-produced, convenience-driven products. However, the allure of homemade shampoo lies in its harmony with nature, its customization potential, and its contribution to a sustainable lifestyle. This chapter delves into the fascinating journey of discovering homemade shampoo and the transformative impact it can have on your hair and your connection with the natural world.

The Appeal of Homemade Shampoo:

Picture this: you're standing in your bathroom, holding a plastic bottle filled with a viscous, brightly colored liquid that promises to cleanse and nourish your hair. The label boasts exotic ingredients, cutting-edge technology, and miraculous results. Yet, you can't help but wonder about the lengthy list of unpronounceable chemicals in the ingredient list. What exactly are you putting on your scalp and hair?

This moment of reflection is where the appeal of homemade shampoo often begins. More and more people are becoming conscious of the chemicals and synthetic additives present in commercial hair care products. The desire for healthier, safer alternatives has sparked an interest in crafting one's shampoo at home, using natural and organic ingredients. Homemade shampoo, at its core, represents a return to simplicity and a conscious choice to be in control of what we put on our bodies.

Understanding the Benefits of Natural Ingredients:

Why choose natural ingredients for your hair care routine? The answer lies in their inherent properties and the benefits they bring to your hair and scalp. Natural ingredients are, in many ways, a throwback to traditional wisdom, where plants, herbs, and oils were used for their therapeutic properties.

Gentleness: One of the most significant advantages of natural ingredients is their gentle nature. Commercial shampoos often contain harsh surfactants like sulfates, which can strip away natural oils from your hair and scalp, leading to dryness and irritation. Natural ingredients, on the other hand, are generally milder and can clean your hair without causing excessive damage.

Nourishment: Natural ingredients are rich in vitamins,

minerals, and antioxidants that can nourish your hair. For instance, coconut oil is known for its moisturizing properties, while aloe vera can soothe an itchy scalp. Using homemade shampoo allows you to harness the natural goodness of these ingredients to promote healthier, shinier hair.

Customization: Everyone's hair is unique, and what works for one person may not work for another. Homemade shampoo offers the exciting opportunity to customize your hair care routine. Whether you have straight, wavy, curly, or coily hair, you can tailor your homemade shampoo recipes to meet your specific needs. Additionally, you can experiment with different ingredients to address issues such as dandruff, excessive oiliness, or hair loss.

Sustainability and Ethical Considerations:

Beyond the personal benefits, homemade shampoo aligns with broader sustainability and ethical considerations. The cosmetics industry is notorious for its environmental impact, with plastic packaging, chemical waste, and animal testing being significant concerns. By making your shampoo at home, you reduce your reliance on plastic bottles and contribute to a more sustainable lifestyle.

Moreover, homemade shampoo often involves using locally sourced, organic, or fair-trade ingredients, supporting small-scale farmers and ethical business practices. This conscious consumerism fosters a deeper connection between you and the producers of these ingredients, reinforcing the sense of community and responsibility towards our planet.

Setting the Stage for a Journey towards Sustainable Hair Care:

As you embark on this journey into the world of homemade shampoo, it's essential to recognize that it's not just about the end product—it's about the process and the lifestyle it represents. It's about reconnecting with the Earth's offerings, honoring time-honored traditions, and making informed choices that resonate with your values.

This book will guide you through the fascinating world of homemade shampoo, from understanding the basics of hair science to formulating recipes for different hair types, and from exploring tools and techniques to transitioning from commercial to homemade shampoo seamlessly. It will also delve into holistic approaches to hair care and emphasize the interconnectedness of self-care, sustainability, and the nurturing touch of nature.

So, whether you're a curious beginner or an experienced naturalist, join us in this exploration of homemade shampoo, and together, let's nurture our hair and the environment, one homemade batch at a time.

CHAPTER 2

The Basics of Hair Science

Hair. We all have it, but how often do we stop and think about what it actually is, how it grows, and why it behaves the way it does? Understanding the fundamentals of hair science is crucial before delving into the world of homemade shampoo. In this chapter, we'll take a deep dive into the biology of your hair, common hair problems, and how homemade shampoo can address specific hair needs.

Hair: More Than Just Strands

Hair might seem like a simple part of our bodies, but it's a complex structure with its own fascinating story. At its core, hair is composed of a protein called keratin, the same protein found in our skin and nails. Each strand of hair grows from a tiny, tube-like hair follicle embedded in our scalp. Hair growth is a continuous cycle, with individual hairs going through phases of growth, rest, and shedding.

Understanding this cycle is crucial for effective hair care. For instance, homemade shampoos can be formulated to promote healthy hair growth and minimize hair loss by providing the essential nutrients that hair follicles need.

The Role of Sebaceous Glands

Our scalps are home to sebaceous glands that produce an oily substance called sebum. Sebum acts as a natural conditioner for our hair, keeping it soft and shiny. However, an overproduction of sebum can lead to oily hair and scalp, while an underproduction can result in dryness and itchiness.

Commercial shampoos often aim to control sebum production, but they can be harsh, stripping away too much sebum and causing the scalp to compensate by producing even more oil. Homemade shampoos, with their milder ingredients, can help balance sebum production more naturally, promoting healthier hair and scalp conditions.

Common Hair Problems and Causes

Before we discuss how homemade shampoo can address specific hair needs, let's explore some of the most common hair problems people face and their underlying causes:

1. **Dandruff:** Dandruff is often caused by a fungal infection on the scalp or by an excessively dry scalp. Homemade shampoos can incorporate ingredients like tea tree oil or aloe vera, which have antifungal and moisturizing properties, respectively, to combat dandruff naturally.

2. **Dry and Damaged Hair:** Environmental factors, heat styling, and chemical treatments can lead to dry and damaged hair. Homemade shampoos can be infused with nourishing ingredients like avocado oil, honey, or shea butter to restore moisture and repair damaged hair.

3. **Hair Loss:** Hair loss can result from various factors, including genetics, hormonal changes, and stress. Homemade shampoos can include ingredients like rosemary essential oil, which

may stimulate hair growth, and castor oil, which can strengthen hair follicles and reduce breakage.

4. **Oily Hair:** An overproduction of sebum can leave hair looking greasy. Homemade shampoos can incorporate natural astringents like witch hazel or lemon juice to help control oiliness without over-drying the scalp.

5. **Scalp Sensitivity:** Some people have sensitive scalps that can become irritated by harsh chemicals in commercial shampoos.

Homemade shampoos, with their gentle and natural ingredients, are often a better choice for those with sensitive skin.

Homemade Shampoo Solutions

Now that we've covered the basics of hair science and common hair problems, let's explore how homemade shampoo can be tailored to address these issues effectively:

1. **Nourishing Ingredients:** Homemade shampoos can be enriched with natural oils

like argan oil, jojoba oil, or coconut oil, which provide essential nutrients to the hair and scalp. These oils can help combat dryness, improve hair texture, and add shine.

2. **Antifungal and Antibacterial Agents:** Ingredients like tea tree oil, neem oil, or aloe vera can be included in homemade shampoos to combat fungal or bacterial infections on the scalp, which may alleviate dandruff and itching.

3. **Hair Growth Stimulants:** Homemade shampoos can

incorporate herbs like rosemary, nettle, or horsetail, known for their potential to stimulate hair growth and strengthen hair follicles.

4. **Moisturizing and Hydrating Ingredients:** Natural humectants like honey, glycerin, and aloe vera can be used to retain moisture in the hair, preventing dryness and brittleness.

5. **pH-Balanced Formulas:** Homemade shampoos can be carefully formulated to maintain the scalp's natural

pH balance, preventing excessive oiliness or dryness.

6. **Gentle Cleansers:** Instead of harsh sulfates found in many commercial shampoos, homemade shampoos often use milder cleansing agents like castile soap or soapwort extract, which clean without stripping the hair of essential oils.

By understanding the science of hair and the underlying causes of common hair problems, you can craft homemade shampoo recipes that cater to your specific needs.

Whether you're looking to promote hair growth, combat dandruff, or simply nourish your hair with natural ingredients, homemade shampoo offers a world of possibilities tailored to your unique hair type and concerns.

As you embark on your journey into homemade shampoo making, keep in mind that the beauty of this process lies in its experimentation and customization. Your hair is as unique as you are, and with the knowledge gained in this chapter, you're well-equipped to create a homemade shampoo that not only cleanses but also pampers your hair in the most natural and effective way possible. In the chapters to come, we'll explore the essential ingredients you can use and provide step-by-step instructions for crafting homemade shampoos that will leave your hair looking and feeling its best.

CHAPTER 3

Essential Ingredients for Homemade Shampoo

Welcome to the exciting world of homemade shampoo crafting! In this chapter, we'll dive into the heart of your DIY hair care adventure: the essential ingredients that will transform your homemade shampoo into a nourishing, cleansing, and aromatic elixir. We'll explore the properties and benefits of natural ingredients, from herbs and oils to essential oils and more. By understanding these components, you'll gain the knowledge needed to create personalized homemade shampoo recipes tailored to your unique hair type and preferences.

1. Natural Oils: The Foundation of Homemade Shampoo

Natural oils are the cornerstone of homemade shampoo. They provide essential nutrients, moisture, and natural cleansing properties for your hair and scalp. Here are some common natural oils used in homemade shampoo:

- **Coconut Oil:** Renowned for its deep moisturizing properties, coconut oil helps prevent protein loss from hair, keeping it healthy and strong.
- **Olive Oil:** Rich in antioxidants and vitamins, olive oil can add shine, softness, and strength to your hair.
- **Jojoba Oil:** This oil closely resembles the natural sebum produced by our scalps, making it an excellent moisturizer and conditioner.
- **Argan Oil:** Known as "liquid gold," argan oil is

packed with vitamins and fatty acids that promote hair elasticity, reduce frizz, and add shine.

- **Castor Oil:** Castor oil is often used to stimulate hair growth and strengthen hair follicles, making it a popular choice for those dealing with hair loss.

- **Avocado Oil:** Abundant in vitamins A, D, and E, avocado oil helps moisturize and nourish hair, leaving it soft and silky.

- **Almond Oil:** Almond oil is a light, non-greasy oil that can add shine and reduce hair breakage.

- **Grapeseed Oil:** This lightweight oil is rich in antioxidants and vitamin E, making it suitable for all hair types, especially fine hair.

2. Herbs and Botanicals: Nature's Medicinal Bounty

Herbs and botanicals have been used for centuries to promote hair health and address specific concerns. They can be infused into your homemade shampoo to harness their natural benefits. Some popular herbs and botanicals for homemade shampoos include:

- **Rosemary:** Rosemary is known for stimulating hair growth, improving circulation in the scalp, and preventing dandruff.
- **Lavender:** Lavender oil has a soothing scent and is often used to promote relaxation. It can also help control dandruff and balance oil production on the scalp.
- **Chamomile:** Chamomile is gentle and calming, making it suitable for sensitive

scalps. It can add shine and lighten hair naturally.

- **Nettle:** Nettle is rich in vitamins and minerals, making it an excellent choice for strengthening hair and reducing hair loss.

- **Aloe Vera:** Aloe vera gel can soothe an itchy scalp, add moisture, and promote hair growth.

- **Hibiscus:** Hibiscus flowers are known for their natural conditioning properties and can add shine and strengthen hair.

- **Calendula:** Calendula petals have anti-inflammatory and soothing properties, making them suitable for sensitive scalps.

- **Peppermint:** Peppermint oil can invigorate the scalp and promote hair growth while providing a refreshing sensation.

3. Essential Oils: Aromatherapy for Your Hair

Essential oils not only add delightful scents to your homemade shampoo but also offer therapeutic benefits for your hair and scalp. When using essential oils, keep in mind that they are highly concentrated, so a few drops go a long way. Some essential oils commonly used in homemade shampoo include:

- **Tea Tree Oil:** Tea tree oil is renowned for its antifungal and antibacterial properties, making it effective in combating dandruff and scalp issues.
- **Lemon Oil:** Lemon oil has a fresh, invigorating scent and can help control oiliness on the scalp.
- **Peppermint Oil:** Besides its invigorating scent, peppermint oil can promote

hair growth and improve scalp health.

- **Lavender Oil:** Lavender oil has a calming scent and is beneficial for dry or sensitive scalps.

- **Rosemary Oil:** Rosemary oil is a go-to choice for stimulating hair growth and improving hair thickness.

- **Cedarwood Oil:** Cedarwood oil is often used to help balance oil production on the scalp and prevent hair loss.

4. Other Natural Ingredients: Customization and Creativity

Beyond oils, herbs, and essential oils, there are various other natural ingredients you can incorporate into your homemade shampoo to customize its properties and benefits. Some examples include:

- **Honey:** Honey is a natural humectant, meaning it helps retain moisture in the hair, making it a fantastic choice for dry hair.
- **Egg:** Eggs are packed with protein and can strengthen hair strands, add shine, and improve overall hair health.

- **Yogurt:** Yogurt is rich in lactic acid, which can cleanse and exfoliate the scalp, promoting a healthy environment for hair growth.

- **Apple Cider Vinegar:** Diluted apple cider vinegar can help balance the scalp's pH, reduce dandruff, and add shine to your hair.

- **Clay (e.g., Rhassoul or Bentonite):** Clays can detoxify the scalp, remove excess oil, and add volume to the hair.

5. Natural Surfactants and Thickeners: Creating the Right Texture

To ensure your homemade shampoo has the right consistency and lather, you can include natural surfactants and thickeners:

- **Castile Soap:** Castile soap is made from plant-based oils and is an excellent natural cleanser for homemade shampoo.

- **Soapwort Extract:** Soapwort is a natural botanical cleanser that can be used to create a gentle foaming action in your shampoo.

- **Xanthan Gum:** Xanthan gum is a natural thickener that can give your shampoo a more gel-like consistency.

- **Guar Gum:** Guar gum is another natural thickener that can add a creamy texture to your shampoo.

Safety Guidelines and Considerations:

While these natural ingredients offer numerous benefits, it's essential to use them safely. Some considerations include:

- **Allergies:** Be mindful of allergies. Perform a patch test before using new ingredients on your scalp to check for adverse reactions.

- **Dilution:** Essential oils should always be diluted in a carrier oil before applying to the skin or scalp to avoid irritation.

- **Quality:** Use high-quality, pure ingredients to ensure the best results and minimize the risk of contaminants.

- **Hygiene:** Ensure your tools and containers are clean when making homemade shampoo to prevent contamination.

By understanding the properties and benefits of these essential ingredients, you're equipped to create homemade shampoo recipes that cater to your specific hair type, concerns, and preferences. In the chapters ahead, we'll explore how to combine these ingredients effectively and provide step-by-step instructions for crafting homemade shampoos that will leave your hair looking, feeling, and smelling fantastic. Get ready to embark on a journey of natural hair care that's as unique as you are.

CHAPTER 4

Recipes for Different Hair Types

In the captivating world of homemade shampoo, one size does not fit all. Just as every person is unique, so is their hair. Hair comes in various textures, and individual needs and concerns vary greatly. This chapter is your guide to creating homemade shampoo recipes tailored to different hair types and specific issues. We'll explore recipes for straight, wavy, curly, and coily hair, each designed to address the unique characteristics and challenges of these hair types.

1. Straight Hair: Nourishing Elegance

Characteristics: Straight hair typically lacks natural volume and tends to be oilier near the scalp.

Recipe for Straight Hair: Gentle Clarifying Shampoo

Ingredients:

- 1/4 cup liquid castile soap
- 1/4 cup distilled water
- 1 tablespoon apple cider vinegar

- 5 drops of lavender essential oil

Instructions:

1. Mix the castile soap and distilled water in a bottle.
2. Add the apple cider vinegar and lavender essential oil.
3. Shake well before each use.
4. Apply a small amount to wet hair, lather, and rinse thoroughly.

2. Wavy Hair: Enhancing Texture

Characteristics: Wavy hair can range from fine to coarse and often falls somewhere between straight and curly. It benefits from products that enhance its natural texture and reduce frizz.

Recipe for Wavy Hair: Coconut Milk Shampoo

Ingredients:

- 1/4 cup coconut milk
- 1/4 cup liquid castile soap
- 1 tablespoon honey
- 5 drops of jasmine essential oil

Instructions:

1. Combine the coconut milk and liquid castile soap in a bottle.

2. Add the honey and jasmine essential oil.
3. Shake well before each use.
4. Apply to wet hair, massage gently, and rinse thoroughly.

3. Curly Hair: Hydrating Curls

Characteristics: Curly hair is often drier due to its unique structure, which makes it more prone to frizz and breakage. Hydration is key.

Recipe for Curly Hair: Avocado and Aloe Vera Shampoo

Ingredients:

- 1/4 ripe avocado
- 1/4 cup aloe vera gel
- 1/4 cup liquid castile soap
- 5 drops of rosemary essential oil

Instructions:

1. Mash the avocado until smooth.
2. Mix in the aloe vera gel and liquid castile soap.
3. Add the rosemary essential oil and blend thoroughly.
4. Apply to wet hair, focusing on the roots and tips, and rinse well.

4. Coily Hair: Moisture-Rich Nourishment

Characteristics: Coily hair is known for its tight curls and can be prone to dryness and breakage. It craves deep moisture and nourishment.

Recipe for Coily Hair: Shea Butter and Jojoba Oil Shampoo

Ingredients:

- 2 tablespoons shea butter
- 2 tablespoons jojoba oil
- 1/4 cup liquid castile soap
- 5 drops of tea tree essential oil

Instructions:

1. Melt the shea butter and jojoba oil together in a double boiler.
2. Once melted, remove from heat and let it cool slightly.
3. Stir in the liquid castile soap and tea tree essential oil.
4. Pour into a bottle and shake well before each use.
5. Apply to wet hair, work into a lather, and rinse thoroughly.

Customization Tips for All Hair Types:

- **Adjust Consistency:** You can adjust the thickness of your shampoo by varying the amount of liquid castile soap or water you use. For thicker shampoo, use less water; for a thinner consistency, use more.

- **Essential Oils:** While the recipes include specific essential oils, feel free to experiment with scents that you prefer. Just ensure that you're using essential oils safe for skin and hair.

- **Frequency:** Homemade shampoo doesn't contain harsh detergents, so it may not lather as much as commercial shampoos. Don't be alarmed; it's still effectively cleansing your hair. You may find that you don't need to shampoo as often, as homemade shampoos are gentler on the scalp.

- **Shelf Life:** Homemade shampoos don't contain synthetic preservatives, so they have a shorter shelf life than commercial products. Store them in a cool, dark place and use them within a few weeks or months, depending on the ingredients used.

- **Transition Period:** If you're transitioning from commercial to homemade shampoo, your hair and scalp may need some time to adjust. Be patient, as it may take a few weeks for your hair to regain its natural balance.

By crafting homemade shampoo recipes tailored to your specific hair type, you're embracing the versatility and personalization that homemade hair care offers. These recipes not only cater to your hair's unique needs but also provide the nourishment and cleansing your hair deserves. As you experiment and find the perfect recipe for your hair, you'll discover the joy of healthier, more vibrant locks, all while minimizing your exposure to synthetic chemicals and embracing a more natural approach to hair care.

In the chapters ahead, we'll continue our journey through the world of homemade shampoo, exploring essential tools and techniques for preparation, providing storage tips, and sharing insights on transitioning from commercial to homemade hair care seamlessly. Get ready to embark on a path to hair care that's as individual as you are.

CHAPTER 5

Tools and Techniques

Welcome to the practical side of your homemade shampoo journey. In this chapter, we'll explore the essential tools and techniques you'll need to craft your homemade shampoo successfully. From sourcing equipment to understanding different preparation methods, this chapter equips you with the knowledge and skills necessary to become a proficient homemade shampoo maker.

Sourcing Equipment for Homemade Shampoo Making:

Before you start mixing up your concoctions, it's essential to have the right tools at your disposal. Here's a list of equipment you'll need for your homemade shampoo-making adventures:

1. **Mixing Bowls:** Invest in a set of glass or stainless steel mixing bowls in various sizes to accommodate different batch sizes.

2. **Measuring Tools:** Precise measurements are crucial in homemade shampoo

making. You'll need measuring cups, spoons, and a kitchen scale.

3. **Whisk or Hand Mixer:** These tools come in handy for blending ingredients and achieving a smooth consistency.

4. **Heat-Resistant Containers:** If your recipe involves heating ingredients, use heat-resistant glass or stainless steel containers for safety.

5. **Funnel:** A funnel helps you transfer your shampoo mixture into bottles without spilling.

6. **Bottles or Containers:** Invest in reusable and eco-friendly glass or plastic bottles with secure caps for storing your homemade shampoo.

7. **Labels:** To avoid confusion, label your bottles with the date of preparation and the ingredients used.

Understanding Different Preparation Methods:

Homemade shampoo can be prepared using various methods, depending on the ingredients and your preferences. Here are three common techniques:

1. **Infusion:** Infusion involves extracting the goodness of herbs or botanicals by steeping them in a liquid, such as water or oil. This method is ideal for extracting the therapeutic properties of herbs and infusing them into your shampoo.

   ○ **Procedure:** Place your chosen herbs or botanicals in a clean glass container and cover them with a liquid (water, oil, or a mixture). Seal the container and allow it to sit in a cool, dark place for several days or weeks. Strain the liquid before using it in your shampoo recipe.

2. **Cold Process:** The cold process method is often used for liquid homemade shampoos. It involves mixing ingredients at room temperature without applying heat.

   o **Procedure:** Combine your chosen ingredients in a mixing bowl, stirring until they're thoroughly blended. Be sure to follow your specific recipe for ingredient order and quantities.

3. **Melt-and-Pour:** This method is suitable for solid bar shampoos or shampoo bars. It involves melting solid ingredients and pouring them into molds to create bars.

   o **Procedure:** Melt your solid ingredients, such as oils and butters, using a double boiler or microwave. Once melted, pour the mixture into molds and allow it to cool and solidify.

Tips for Successful Homemade Shampoo Making:

1. **Sanitization:** Ensure that all your tools and containers are clean and free from any residues. Any contaminants can affect the quality and shelf life of your homcmade shampoo.

2. **Precision in Measurement:** Accuracy in measuring your ingredients is vital. Even small variations can

significantly impact the effectiveness of your shampoo.

3. **Safety Precautions:** When working with heat or essential oils, prioritize safety. Use appropriate safety gear and follow safety guidelines for handling hot ingredients or essential oils.

4. **Stirring and Mixing:** Proper mixing is crucial to ensure that all ingredients are evenly distributed. Use a whisk or hand mixer when necessary to achieve a smooth, uniform texture.

5. **Storage:** Store your homemade shampoo in a cool, dark place to preserve its freshness. If your shampoo contains natural preservatives like vitamin E or certain essential oils (e.g., tea tree oil or lavender oil), it may extend the shelf life.

Transitioning from Commercial to Homemade Shampoo:

Transitioning from commercial shampoos to homemade alternatives can be a gradual process. Here are some tips to make the transition smoother:

1. **Clarifying Shampoo:** Before making the switch, consider using a clarifying shampoo to remove any residue from commercial products. This will help your hair adjust more quickly to homemade shampoo.

2. **Adjust Expectations:** Homemade shampoos may not lather as much as commercial ones due to the absence of sulfates. Don't be concerned; this is normal, and the shampoo is still cleaning your hair effectively.

3. **Balancing Your Scalp:** If your scalp produces excess oil initially, don't fret. It's adjusting to the milder ingredients in homemade shampoo. Over time, your scalp's oil production should balance out.

4. **Experiment:** Be open to experimentation as you find the homemade shampoo recipe that works best for your hair type and specific needs. You can always tweak your recipe until it suits you perfectly.

Conclusion: Empowering Your Hair Care Journey

As you delve into the practical aspects of homemade shampoo making, you're taking a significant step toward a more sustainable and personalized hair care routine. By sourcing the right equipment, mastering different preparation methods, and following safety guidelines, you're well-prepared to create homemade shampoos that cater to your unique hair needs.

Homemade shampoo not only benefits your hair but also connects you more deeply to the natural world. You become a conscious consumer, aware of the ingredients you use and their impact on your hair and the environment. Additionally, you gain the satisfaction of crafting your hair care products, knowing exactly what goes into them.

In the chapters ahead, we'll continue our exploration of homemade shampoo, delving into the art of crafting recipes for specific hair types and addressing common hair concerns. You'll discover the joy of customizing your hair care routine, all while fostering a deeper connection to the beauty of natural ingredients and sustainable living. Get ready to embark on a hair care journey that's as empowering as it is fulfilling.

CHAPTER 6

Transitioning to Homemade Shampoo

Congratulations on your journey into the world of homemade shampoo! As you start exploring the possibilities of crafting your own hair care products, you may be wondering how to transition from commercial shampoos to your new homemade routine. This chapter is your guide to making that transition smoothly and effectively. We'll explore the adjustment period, potential challenges, and share success stories from individuals who've embraced homemade shampoo.

The Adjustment Period: What to Expect

Transitioning from commercial shampoos to homemade alternatives can be an exciting yet challenging process. It's essential to understand that your hair and scalp may need some time to adapt to the milder, more natural ingredients in homemade shampoo. Here's what to expect during the adjustment period:

1. **Oil Imbalance:** Initially, your scalp may overproduce oil as it adapts to the gentler cleansing action of homemade shampoo. This can make your hair feel greasier than usual.

2. **Less Lather:** Homemade shampoos typically produce less lather compared to commercial ones because they lack sulfates, which create abundant foam. Don't be alarmed if your homemade shampoo doesn't foam up as much; it's still effectively cleansing your hair.

3. **Detox Period:** Some individuals experience a "detox" period during the transition. Your hair may feel waxy, heavy, or lifeless as it releases built-up residues from commercial products. This is a temporary phase and a sign that your homemade shampoo is working to remove these residues.

4. **Adjusting to Ingredients:** Each homemade shampoo recipe is unique, so it may take a few tries to find the one that

suits your hair type and specific needs best.

Tips for a Smooth Transition:

1. **Clarifying Shampoo:** Before making the switch, consider using a clarifying shampoo to remove any buildup from commercial products. This will prepare your hair for the transition.

2. **Gradual Transition:** If you're unsure about diving straight into homemade shampoo, consider using it every other wash. This allows your hair to adapt more gradually.

3. **Vinegar Rinse:** An occasional apple cider vinegar rinse can help balance your scalp's pH, making the transition smoother.

4. **Adjust Expectations:** Be patient and realistic about your expectations. Your hair may not look or feel perfect during the transition, but this phase is temporary.

Overcoming Challenges:

Transitioning to homemade shampoo isn't always without its challenges. Here are some common issues you may encounter and how to address them:

1. **Greasy Hair:** If your hair feels greasy during the transition, you can extend the time between washes, use a dry shampoo, or rinse your hair with diluted apple cider vinegar to help balance oil production.

2. **Detox Phase:** If you experience the waxy or heavy feeling associated with the detox phase, be patient. Your hair will improve as it continues to adjust to the new routine.

3. **Finding the Right Recipe:** It may take some experimentation to find the homemade shampoo recipe that works best for your hair type and needs. Don't be afraid to try different recipes until you find your perfect match.

4. **Styling Products:** Homemade shampoos may not always remove heavy styling products completely. Consider using natural styling products that are easier to wash out, or use a clarifying shampoo occasionally.

Success Stories: Embracing Homemade Shampoo

To inspire and reassure you on your homemade shampoo journey, here are two success stories from individuals who've embraced homemade hair care:

Sarah's Story: From Dry and Brittle to Lustrous Locks

Sarah had struggled with dry, brittle hair for years. She'd tried various commercial shampoos and conditioners, but nothing seemed to work. Frustrated by the chemicals in these products, she decided to explore homemade shampoo.

Sarah began with a simple homemade shampoo recipe featuring coconut milk, liquid castile soap, honey, and lavender essential oil. She noticed that her hair felt softer and more manageable after just a few washes. The transition was a bit challenging as her hair adjusted, but she persevered. Over time, her hair regained its natural shine and strength.

Today, Sarah continues to experiment with different homemade shampoo recipes, customizing them to her hair's changing needs. She not only enjoys healthier hair but also the satisfaction of knowing exactly what goes into her hair care products.

David's Story: Nurturing Curls Naturally

David had curly hair that was prone to frizz and dryness. He had relied on commercial products that promised to tame his curls, but they left his hair feeling weighed down and lifeless. David wanted a more natural solution that embraced his hair's natural texture.

After researching homemade shampoo recipes for curly hair, David started using an avocado and aloe vera shampoo. He found that this homemade alternative provided deep moisture and enhanced his curls' definition. David also began using natural styling products that worked in harmony with his homemade shampoo.

Today, David's curls are more vibrant and healthy than ever before. He's proud to have embraced a hair care routine that not only nurtures his curls but also aligns with his values of sustainability and natural living.

Conclusion: Embrace the Transition

Transitioning to homemade shampoo is a journey that can lead to healthier, more vibrant hair and a stronger connection to natural ingredients. While the adjustment period may present some challenges, it's a small price to pay for the long-term benefits of using gentler, chemical-free hair care products.

Remember that your hair is unique, and the transition may

vary from person to person. Be patient, stay open to experimentation, and don't hesitate to seek advice and support from the growing community of homemade shampoo enthusiasts.

In the chapters ahead, we'll continue to explore the world of homemade shampoo, from customizing recipes to exploring holistic approaches to hair care. Your journey is just beginning, and with each step, you're nurturing both your hair and your connection to the beauty of natural living. Embrace the transition, and let your hair shine in its natural, healthy glory.

CHAPTER 7

Holistic Hair Care and Beyond

Congratulations on your journey into the world of homemade shampoo! By now, you've gained a deeper understanding of your hair, explored essential ingredients, mastered the art of crafting homemade shampoos, and navigated the transition from commercial to homemade hair care. In this chapter, we'll take your hair care journey to the next level by delving into the holistic aspects of hair care and exploring ways to elevate your homemade hair care routine.

The Holistic Approach to Hair Care:

Holistic hair care goes beyond just the products you use. It involves nurturing your hair from the inside out, considering the impact of lifestyle, diet, and mindfulness on the health and vitality of your locks. Here are some key aspects of holistic hair care:

1. Nutrition: Feeding Your Hair From Within

Your hair, like the rest of your body, thrives on proper nutrition. A diet rich in vitamins, minerals, and essential fatty acids can promote hair growth, strength, and overall health. Consider incorporating these hair-friendly foods into your meals:

- **Protein:** Hair is primarily composed of a protein called keratin. Incorporate lean protein sources like poultry, fish, beans, and tofu into your diet.

- **Omega-3 Fatty Acids:** These healthy fats are found in fish, flaxseeds, and walnuts and can help prevent dry and brittle hair.

- **Vitamins:** Vitamins like Biotin (B7), Vitamin E, and Vitamin C are essential for hair health. You can find these in foods like eggs, nuts, leafy greens, and citrus fruits.

- **Iron:** Iron deficiency can lead to hair loss. Consume iron-rich foods such as spinach, lentils, and red meat.

- **Water:** Staying hydrated is crucial for maintaining the moisture balance of your hair and scalp.

2. Stress Management: Mind-Body Connection

Stress can impact your hair health. Chronic stress can lead to hair loss or thinning. Incorporating stress-reduction techniques into your daily routine, such as meditation, yoga, or mindfulness exercises, can help improve your hair's overall condition.

3. Scalp Health: The Foundation of Beautiful Hair

A healthy scalp is essential for healthy hair. Consider incorporating scalp massages into your routine to improve blood circulation and promote hair growth. You can use natural oils like coconut or jojoba oil for these massages. Scalp exfoliation, done gently, can also remove dead skin cells and promote a healthier scalp.

4. Sleep and Hair Health: The Restorative Power of Rest

Getting enough sleep is essential for overall health, including hair health. During sleep, your body repairs and regenerates, and this includes your hair. Aim for 7-9 hours of quality sleep per night to support your hair's natural growth cycle.

Elevating Your Homemade Shampoo Routine:

Now that we've covered the holistic aspects of hair care, let's explore how to enhance your homemade shampoo routine for even more remarkable results:

1. Pre-Shampoo Treatments:

Consider incorporating pre-shampoo treatments into your routine to address specific hair concerns. Here are a few options:

- **Hot Oil Treatment:** Warm up natural oils like coconut, olive, or argan oil and massage them into your hair and scalp. Leave it on for at least 30 minutes before shampooing.

- **Hair Masks:** Homemade hair masks using ingredients like avocado, egg, honey, or yogurt can provide deep conditioning and nourishment.

2. Herbal Rinses:

Herbal rinses can be used after shampooing to add shine, improve hair texture, and address specific concerns. Some popular herbal rinses include:

- **Rosemary Rinse:** Rosemary stimulates hair growth and adds shine.
- **Chamomile Rinse:** Chamomile soothes the scalp and can lighten hair naturally.
- **Nettle Rinse:** Nettle strengthens hair and reduces hair loss.
- **Hibiscus Rinse:** Hibiscus adds shine and conditions the hair.

To prepare a herbal rinse, steep the chosen herbs in hot water, strain, and use the infused water as a final rinse after shampooing.

3. pH Balancing:

Consider using an apple cider vinegar (ACV) rinse as a final step in your hair care routine. ACV helps balance the pH of your hair and scalp, leaving it smooth and shiny. Dilute ACV with water (usually 1-2 tablespoons of ACV in 1 cup of water) and pour it over your hair as a final rinse. Be sure to rinse it out thoroughly.

4. Minimal Heat Styling:

Limit the use of heat styling tools like hairdryers, straighteners, and curling irons. Excessive heat can damage your hair, making it more prone to breakage and dryness. If you must use heat, apply a heat protectant product before styling.

5. Trimming:

Regular hair trims can help prevent split ends and maintain the overall health of your hair. Aim for a trim every 6-8 weeks, or as needed.

Conclusion: A Holistic Journey to Radiant Hair

Embracing a holistic approach to hair care is a journey that combines self-care, nutrition, mindfulness, and the power of natural ingredients. By nurturing your hair from within and enhancing your homemade shampoo routine with pre-shampoo treatments, herbal rinses, and pH-balancing steps, you're elevating your hair care to new heights.

As you continue your homemade shampoo journey, remember that it's not just about achieving beautiful hair; it's about embracing a lifestyle that values self-care, sustainability, and natural living. Your hair care routine becomes a ritual, a way to connect with yourself and the world around you.

In the chapters ahead, we'll explore advanced homemade hair care techniques, share expert tips on maintaining healthy hair, and delve into the benefits of embracing a natural lifestyle for your overall well-being. Your journey to radiant, healthy hair is an ongoing adventure, and with each step, you're nurturing both your hair and your connection to the beauty of holistic living. Embrace the journey, and let your hair shine in its natural, healthy glory.

CHAPTER 8

Expert Tips and Sustainable Living

As you've embarked on your homemade shampoo journey and explored various aspects of holistic hair care, you've gained valuable knowledge about crafting your own hair care products and nurturing your hair from the inside out. In this final chapter, we'll delve into expert tips and sustainable living practices to help you further refine your homemade hair care routine and make mindful choices that benefit both your hair and the planet.

Expert Tips for Homemade Hair Care:

1. **Quality Ingredients:** Invest in high-quality, organic, and sustainably sourced ingredients for your homemade shampoos. The quality of your ingredients can significantly impact the effectiveness of your hair care products.

2. **Customization:** Experiment with different ingredients, essential oils, and herbs to tailor your

homemade shampoo to your unique hair type and concerns. Keep a journal to track your experiments and results.

3. **Balanced Formulas:** Create balanced formulas that address cleansing, moisturizing, and nourishing aspects of hair care. Understanding the role of each ingredient in your recipe is essential for achieving the desired results.

4. **Avoid Overwashing:** Homemade shampoos are gentler and don't strip your hair of natural oils as

commercial products might. Avoid overwashing your hair, which can lead to dryness and irritation. Listen to your hair's needs and wash accordingly.

5. **pH Awareness:** Pay attention to the pH of your homemade shampoo. Hair and scalp have a slightly acidic pH, and maintaining this balance is crucial for hair health. Ingredients like apple cider vinegar can help balance pH.

6. **Patience During Transition:** Be patient as your hair transitions from

commercial to homemade shampoo. It may take time for your hair to adjust, but the results are worth the effort.

7. **Cold Water Rinse:** Finish your shampooing with a cold water rinse. Cold water can help seal the hair cuticles, making your hair smoother and shinier.

Sustainable Living Practices:

1. **Reduce, Reuse, Recycle:** Embrace the mantra of sustainability by reducing waste, reusing containers, and recycling materials

whenever possible. Glass containers used for your homemade shampoo can often be reused for new batches or for storing other products.

2. **Zero Waste Packaging:** Look for zero-waste or eco-friendly packaging options when purchasing ingredients for your homemade shampoo. Buy in bulk to reduce packaging waste.

3. **Mindful Consumption:** Be a conscious consumer by choosing products and ingredients that align with your values. Support brands

that prioritize sustainability and ethical practices.

4. **Natural Cleaning:** Extend your sustainable living practices to other areas of your life. Explore natural cleaning solutions, such as using baking soda and vinegar, to reduce the environmental impact of conventional cleaning products.

5. **Energy Efficiency:** Practice energy efficiency at home by using LED bulbs, unplugging devices when not in use, and optimizing your

home's heating and cooling systems.

6. **Cruelty-Free and Vegan Choices:** If you're an advocate for animal welfare, choose ingredients and products that are cruelty-free and vegan, meaning they haven't been tested on animals and contain no animal-derived ingredients.

Sharing Your Knowledge:

As you continue your homemade hair care journey and incorporate sustainable living practices into your life, consider sharing your knowledge and experiences with others. Here are some ways you can inspire and educate those around you:

1. **Social Media:** Use platforms like Instagram, TikTok, or YouTube to share your homemade hair care routines, recipes, and sustainability tips. Engage with a community of like-minded individuals and learn from others.

2. **Blogging or Vlogging:** Start a blog or vlog dedicated to natural living, holistic hair care, and sustainable practices. Document your

journey, share your insights, and connect with a global audience.

3. **Local Workshops:** Host workshops or classes in your local community to teach others how to make homemade hair care products or adopt sustainable living practices. These can be fun and interactive opportunities to connect with others.

4. **Online Communities:** Join online forums, groups, or communities focused on natural hair care and sustainability. Share your

experiences and learn from others who share your interests.

5. **Eco-Friendly Initiatives:** Participate in or initiate eco-friendly initiatives in your community, such as clean-up events, recycling drives, or sustainable living fairs.

CONCLUSION

A Sustainable, Holistic Journey

Your homemade hair care journey has taken you on a path of self-discovery, natural living, and mindful choices. By crafting your own hair care products, embracing holistic practices, and adopting sustainable living habits, you're not only nurturing your hair but also contributing to a healthier planet.

Remember that your journey is ongoing, and there is always more to learn and explore. Continue to experiment with homemade shampoo recipes, fine-tune your holistic approach to hair care, and discover new ways to live sustainably. By doing so, you're creating a life that aligns with your values, respects the environment, and fosters a deeper connection with the beauty of natural living.

In closing, your homemade hair care journey is a testament to the power of self-care, knowledge, and conscious choices. Your hair shines with the radiance of health, and your lifestyle reflects a commitment to a better world. May your path be filled with beauty, wellness, and sustainability, and may your journey inspire others to embark on their own holistic, sustainable adventures.